# winter wedding

**6**

### day

**X** Only the bride should wear white

Black opaque tights should never be worn with white

Don't opt for the standard "wedding hat." Go for something more jaunty

Looks like a uniform for the mature lady

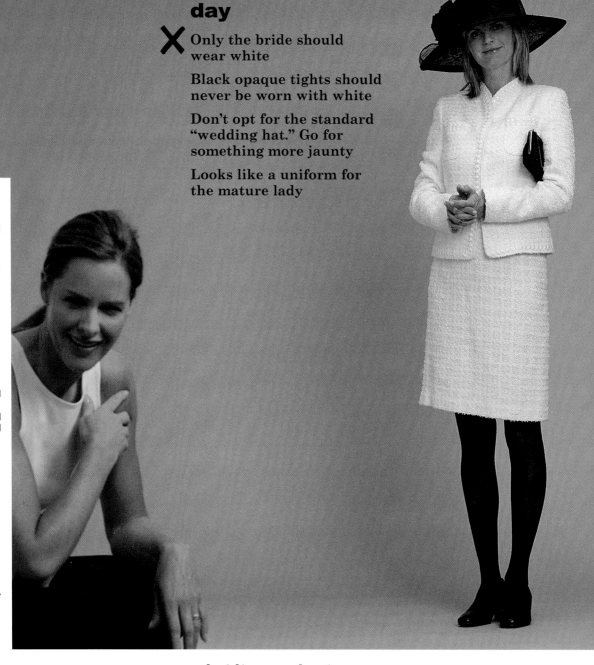

### what it says about you

"I feel safe in the pigeonhole of middle age. It's not often that I dress up because I don't get out much these days."

## day

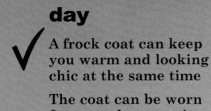

✓ **A frock coat can keep you warm and looking chic at the same time**

**The coat can be worn for everyday occasions as well**

**Elegant, flat leather boots help you navigate any dirty country lanes**

**A sharp hat is best shown off with simple tailoring**

**what it says about you**

"Oh, this is something I threw on at the last minute. But I can bring it together because I understand the importance of good tailoring."

### day

**✗** Looking trendy is not about wearing work clothes to a wedding

A suede skirt and suede jacket should never be worn together – whether they match or not

Even if you don't wear a hat you should still look as though you've made an effort

### what it says about you

"This suit is so useful that I've worn it to death. I have no sense of occasion and know my friends love me anyway for my personality."

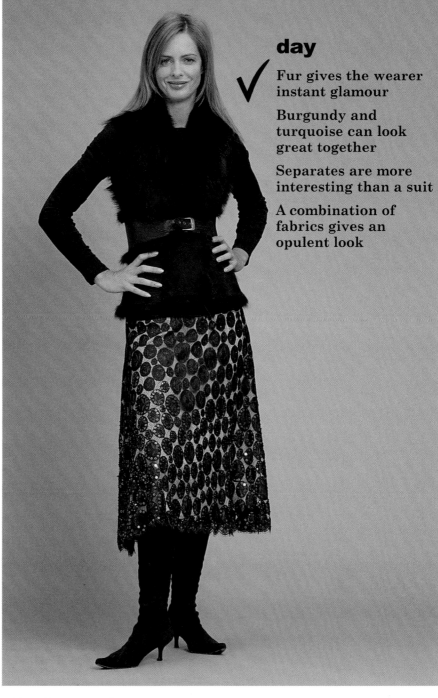

## day

✓ Fur gives the wearer instant glamour

Burgundy and turquoise can look great together

Separates are more interesting than a suit

A combination of fabrics gives an opulent look

### what it says about you

"My life is too full to have the time to buy a special wedding outfit. And it's not necessary because I'm versatile by nature. I can fit in anywhere and love talking to anyone so I'm the ideal wedding guest."

## evening

✗ A huge coat overpowers what's underneath and takes all the elegance out of an outfit

Open-toed sandals look wrong with the coat (and your feet will freeze)

All black is safe – but very uninspiring

**winter wedding smart**

### what it says about you

"I'm a very creative person, with a passion for cats and street art. My star sign is Virgo with Aries rising and I have a colonic once a month."

# evening

✓ A fitted jacket and long skirt flatter most figures and give a long lean silhouette

Wearing a printed skirt and a darker jacket is good if you are bigger up top (try the reverse if you are bigger down below)

Later, the jacket can be removed to show off a black-tie outfit

## what it says about you

"I respect the seriousness of the marriage vows; yet I intend to let my hair down at the party without disturbing my outfit. If you're lucky I'll whip off my jacket to reveal a little more."

winter wedding trendy

## evening

X Black cheapens the vibrancy of the skirt

Fur hat is too daytime

An ankle-skimming skirt looks the wrong length with kitten-heeled boots

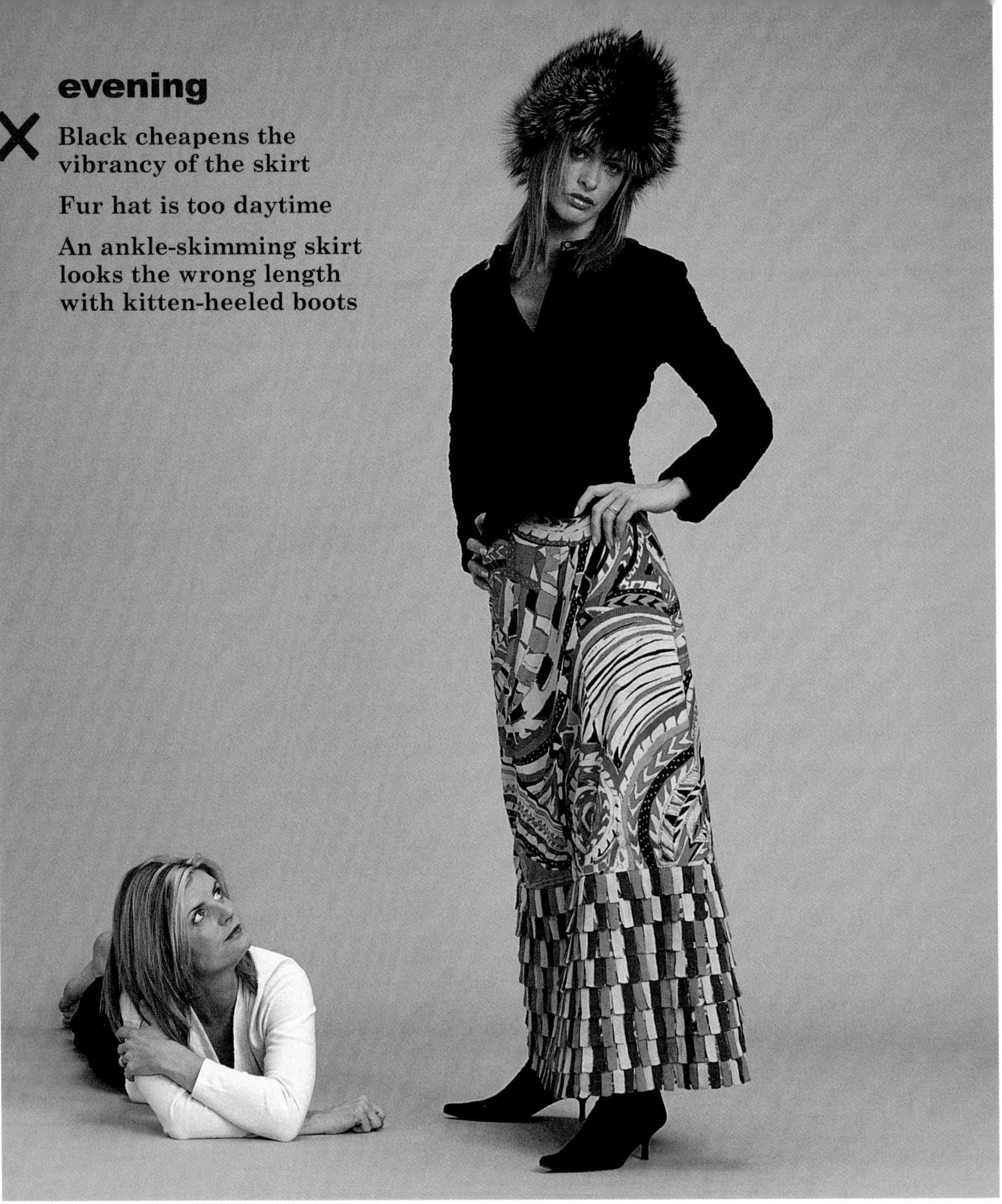

**what it says about you**

"My hat is from Prada, the jacket McQueen, the skirt Missoni, boots by Stephane Kélian. I love YSL and think Tom Ford is a genius… I'm not boring you am I?"

## evening

✓ This demonstrates how mixing designer, vintage and of-the-moment works well

Mixing patterns succeeds when the same colors are used

A long skirt looks great with high heels that cannot be seen

### what it says about you

"Fashion is my passion, but I keep my clothing sources to myself. You certainly won't be bored by me at dinner and if you're stuck for something to say, tell me you adore my butterflies."

## winter wedding/day

**smart**

| $ | $$ | $$$ |
|---|----|-----|
| Zara, H & M, Macy's, Anthropologie **Accessories** Claire's, Steven Madden, Macy's | Nicole Miller, BCBG, Laundry, Catherine Malandrino, Vanessa Bruno, Nanette Lepore **Accessories** Nicole Miller, BCBG, Charles Jourdan, Joseph | Chloé, Prada, Missoni, Temperley, Alberta Ferretti, Vivienne Westwood **Accessories** Christian Louboutin, Hermès |

**trendy**

| $ | $$ | $$$ |
|---|----|-----|
| Zara, Macy's, H & M, Anthropologie, Banana Republic **Accessories** Zara, Banana Republic, Anthropologie | Nicole Miller, BCBG, Marc by Marc Jacobs, Diane von Furstenberg, Joseph **Accessories** Nicole Miller, BCBG, Kenneth Cole, Joseph | Temperley, Alberta Ferretti, Jimmy Choo, Sigerson Morrison, MaxMara **Accessories** Fendi, Jimmy Choo, Sigerson Morrison |

## winter wedding/evening

**smart**

| $ | $$ | $$$ |
|---|----|-----|
| Zara, H & M, Macy's, Gap Body, Banana Republic, Club Monaco **Accessories** Claire's, Banana Republic, Zara | Nicole Miller, Betsey Johnson, Diane von Furstenberg, BCBG, Dosa **Accessories** Agatha, BCBG, Nicole Miller | Dries van Noten, Chloé, Vivienne Westwood, Armani, Yves Saint Laurent, Temperley, Emanuel Ungaro, Alberta Ferretti, Escada **Accessories** Jimmy Choo, Erickson Beamon, Christian Louboutin |

**trendy**

| $ | $$ | $$$ |
|---|----|-----|
| Zara, Urban Outfitters, Club Monaco, Banana Republic, Express **Accessories** Zara, Banana Republic, Express | Marc by Marc Jacobs, Development, Nicole Miller, Catherine Malandrino, BCBG **Accessories** Marc by Marc Jacobs, Cynthia Rowley, Christian Dior | Etro, Chloé, Missoni, Alberta Ferretti, Ungaro, Costume National **Accessories** Moschino, Erickson Beamon, Philip Treacy |

# winter wedding

- Combine colors as nature intended. Think of the colors of leaves in autumn. Nothing jars

- Don't wear black to a wedding

- If it's really cold, consider wearing thermals underneath your outfit instead of a heavy coat that will only hide all the effort you've made

- Remember gloves keep you warm and add an element of elegance – as long as they are not black and woolly

- Check that the shadow from your hat does not accentuate the dark circles under your eyes

- Blush is even more important in winter, especially if you suffer from a sallow complexion

- Even if it's a Christmassy wedding, don't go over-the-top glitzy on the makeup

- If hose are involved in an outfit and you're in a potentially splintery church, carry a spare pair

tips

**summer holiday** The thought of having to step into a bikini fills all but the mad with a fit of panic. The thought of our pallid bodies emerging on the beach as radiating beacons of mottled skin, further defaced by cellulite-infested thighs, is enough to send us into eternal seclusion. Tabloids expound miracle "Bikini Diets" and magazines tell us how to achieve a polished bronze hide, the underlying message being that your body has to be marble hard, size Stupidly Thin and golden brown before venturing anywhere near the ghastly swimsuit. Oh please. What crap. No wonder we all feel such trepidation before stripping off in public. But there are ways and means to cover bad bits in a nonchalant fashion, just as there are fabulous beach looks that detract any onlookers from your lack of tan and tone. In a weird way people are far more likely to notice a disgusting swimsuit than they are a saggy arse. Once the sun goes down it's easy to look carefree and informally stylish. This can be achieved with old friends you've had in your closet for years – just be sure they aren't frumpy, dated or too over the top. Have a good one and don't forget to send us a postcard!

# summer holiday

7

## on the beach

✗ Diamonds with swim-suits are a figment of Jackie Collins's imagination

Although black can be slimming, when teamed with gold sandals and jewelry it's too Palm Beach

Too much makeup will only run when the sun gets hot

### what it says about you

"I killed off all five of my previous husbands and was wondering if you were rich enough to be the next? My beauty is only as thick as my makeup."

## on the beach

✓

A coordinated sarong and swimsuit works if the print is small and unobtrusive

Uniformity of pattern and color is slimming and elongates the body

Flat gold sandals are glamorous without looking tarty

### what it says about you

"I'm discreet and don't like attracting attention, but I'll be warm and friendly if you want to chat with me."

## on the beach

**X**

High-waisted, gathered shorts flatter no tummies

Shorts are best with a bikini top

Practical sandals look as if they're for the orthopedically impaired

Trust us when we say her butt looks vast in these shorts

### what it says about you

"I don't travel very well. My stomach can't take foreign muck so I make my own sandwiches and bring them to the beach in tidy little Tupperware boxes."

# on the beach

✓ **Low-waisted, flat-fronted longer shorts are the most flattering shape to wear. Team with a bikini top**

**Slip-on shoes are comfortable and flattering to the foot**

**Straw hat is simple but effective**

### what it says about you

"You'll have no idea whether I'm stinking rich or a pauper. I could own the most beautiful villa on the island or be sleeping under canvas on a camping site. You won't care either way 'cause I'm fab."

## on the beach

✗ Wearing everything from one label only accentuates a lack of taste

The bikini on its own would work with some contrasting accessories

Leave scarves to Greek widows or girls in their teens and twenties

### what it says about you

"I think designer labels make me more interesting as a person. The truth is that I have no personality but since I'm easy meat after a few margaritas, who cares?"

## on the beach

✓ A simple swimsuit covered by an exotic wrap makes a statement while covering parts of the body that you'd rather weren't seen when you come out of the water

Looks good and makes a security blanket for those with cellulite and pale skin

### what it says about you

"I can't be bothered with all those high-pressure bikini diets in the tabloids. I just cover up my dodgy bits with something fabulously ethnic."

## after sun

X Black for a summer evening can look too heavy

...especially when teamed with black leather shoes

Polyester fabrics make you sweat like pork in plastic

### what it says about you

"I am a tourist. I refuse to be adventurous and won't stray from the main drag of fast food outlets and tacky tourist shops."

## after sun

✓ Dress is shapely but has no tight waistband to dig into the flesh and exacerbate the pain of sunburnt skin

Gold sandals go with every summer evening outfit

Pale colors make the most of even the faintest tan

### what it says about you

"Stand next to me to keep cool. My holiday has wound me down to the point where I can truly enjoy the bliss of taking time out."

## after sun

✗ Heavy skirt and frumpy T-shirt make you look like you're about to do the weekend shop

Tucked-in top will make you feel hot and look bloated

Don't take a big black bag on a summer holiday or you might be tempted to use it

These shoes scream "varicose veins and bunions"

### what it says about you

"This is my first time abroad and as I'm such a novice traveler, my bag and I are open to every mugger and pickpocket on the beach."

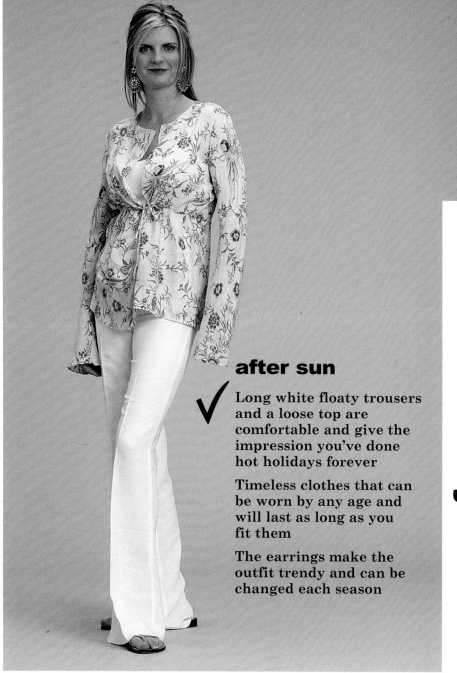

## after sun

✓

**Long white floaty trousers and a loose top are comfortable and give the impression you've done hot holidays forever**

**Timeless clothes that can be worn by any age and will last as long as you fit them**

**The earrings make the outfit trendy and can be changed each season**

### what it says about you

"Where am I staying? Oh no, I live here. And if I really take to you, I'll tell you about this wonderful little bar where all the locals go."

## after sun

✗ Too much makeup on a tanned face makes it look dirty

Very high heels can make ankles and feet swell even more in the heat

Manmade fabrics turn skin into a swampy breeding ground for body odor

**summer holiday trendy**

### what it says about you

"Micro-minis are very in, which is great 'cause I can show off my mahogany tan. Getting a tan is all I really care about and I'm prepared to go to any lengths in self-humiliation to show it off."

## after sun

✓ Silk is the coolest fabric to wear after a long day of sun

Pale colors take the red out of sunburnt skin

A long skirt covers up pale legs if the tan hasn't set in

Flat sandals look good with a long skirt

It only takes one signature piece of clothing to look cool

### what it says about you

"I don't need to roast myself on the beach. I'm just naturally golden all year round and so cool."

## summer holiday/on the beach

| | $ | $$ | $$$ |
|---|---|---|---|
| **smart** | J. Crew, Club Monaco, Guess, H & M, Banana Republic<br>**Accessories**<br>Club Monaco, Zara, Claire's, H & M | French Connection, Miu Miu, Olive and Bette's, BCBG, Alice + Olivia<br>**Accessories**<br>Cacharel, Miu Miu, Olive and Bette's | Prada, La Perla, Missoni, Versace, Celine, Emilio Pucci, Escada Sport, Armani<br>**Accessories**<br>Sigerson Morrison, Emilio Pucci, Gucci |
| **casual** | H & M, Urban Outfitters, Benetton, Adidas, Gap, Abercrombie & Fitch<br>**Accessories**<br>H & M, Claire's, Gap | Diesel, French Connection, Nike, Puma, Juicy Couture<br>**Accessories**<br>Nike, Puma, Birkenstock | Missoni, Marni, Maharishi<br>Prada Sport<br>**Accessories**<br>Nuala, Hogan, Kate Spade, Tod's |
| **trendy** | H & M, Urban Outfitters, Guess, Gap<br>**Accessories**<br>H & M, Urban Outfitters, Girlshop, Target | Paul & Joe, French Connection, BCBG, Cacharel, Alice + Olivia, Juicy Couture<br>**Accessories**<br>French Connection, Sara James, BCBG | Missoni, Emilio Pucci, Chloé, Allegra Hicks, Louis Vuitton, Ann-Louise Roswald, Tuleh<br>**Accessories**<br>Costume National, Pippa Small, Anya Hindmarch |

## summer holiday/after sun

| | $ | $$ | $$$ |
|---|---|---|---|
| **smart** | Zara, H & M, Banana Republic, Club Monaco<br>**Accessories**<br>Zara, H & M, Claire's | French Connection, Nicole Miller, Laundry, Olive and Bette's, Cynthia Rowley, Joseph<br>**Accessories**<br>Longchamp, Nicole Miller, Olive and Bette's | Costume National, Missoni, Alberta Ferretti, Celine, Prada, Escada<br>**Accessories**<br>Jimmy Choo, Manolo Blahnik, Sigerson Morrison |
| **casual** | Gap, H & M, Zara, Express, Macy's, Target, J. Crew, Abercrombie & Fitch<br>**Accessories**<br>J. Crew, Target, Urban Outfitters | French Connection, Juicy Couture, Blue Cult, Punk Royal<br>**Accessories**<br>Diesel, Hervé Chapelier, BCBG | Marni, Vanessa Bruno, Maharishi, Missoni<br>**Accessories**<br>Anya Hindmarch, Pippa Small, Me & Ro, Erickson Beamon |
| **trendy** | Zara, H & M, Urban Outfitters, Club Monaco, Girlshop<br>**Accessories**<br>Claire's, Urban Outfitters, Banana Republic | French Connection, Cacharel, BCBG, Marc by Marc Jacobs<br>**Accessories**<br>BCBG, Marc by Marc Jacobs, Puma | Temperley, Missoni, Miu Miu, Emilio Pucci, Roberto Cavalli, Celine, Marni<br>**Accessories**<br>Christian Louboutin, Sigerson Morrison, Chloé, Me & Ro, Pippa Small, Erickson Beamon |

**where to shop**

# summer holiday

- Make an effort to get your eyelashes tinted so you can avoid the panda look when you're in the water

- If you get your hair colored, do it at least a week before to avoid drastic over-lifting by sun, sea and chlorine

- If you're going to have a fake tan, get it applied a couple of days before so if you wake up to a streaky situation you have time to remove it. St. Tropez does an excellent remover

- Get waxing done at least a couple of days before so your skin has time to calm down

- Don't forget to wax your toes if you're a hairy girl (like Trinny) and belly button (if you're dark haired and it travels)

- If you're a sun worshipper, have a good old exfoliation before you go to remove any dead skin cell barriers to a gorgeous even tan

- If you tend to burn, don't pack any red or pink, as they will only show up your lack of expertise with the SPFs

- Decant favored luxury items into small plastic containers so you can fit even more beauty products into your suitcase. Check out The Container Store, Muji, and Rite Aid for great containers.

- Add mosquito repellent to your aftersun lotion so you never forget to apply some when there's a possibility of being bitten

- When you get home, make a list of everything you didn't wear and don't take them next time if the climate and social situation are the same

**tips**

**winter holiday** Those of you who ski year in, year out will no doubt have gotten the vexed question of what to wear both on and off the slopes down to a fine art. Instead of traveling with 35 suitcases, you limit your baggage to one neat carryall and a piece of hand luggage. You will know how to dress according to your downhill handicap. You won't be fooled by a beginner who's trussed up like Frans Klammer because the combination of professional clothing and quivering snow-plow makes her look ridiculous as opposed to well . . . a beginner. If, though, you're a novice to the game you will quickly discover that gathering together a ski kit must be organized with scientific precision. It's no good just packing a load of heavy woollen goods and chucking in your favorite little black dress. You have to consider the freezing temperatures, hazardous walking conditions and how much cleavage the ski-club can take. You must take into account your skill – or lack of it – as a skier. When you're starting out, you may spend more time on the ground than on your skis, so a double-glazed ski-suit that keeps the snow from sneaking in when you fall can be a godsend.

# winter holiday

8

## on the slopes/ professional

✗ Tight salopettes are only practical for spring skiing

A short, fitted jacket might make your legs look longer, but does nothing to keep you warm

Outfit too restricting for vigorous movement

**what it says about you**

"I'm a fabulous skier, have an amazing figure and no one comes close to me on the slopes – in fact, I'm cold and very uncomfortable."

## on the slopes/ professional

✓ Jacket is roomy enough for adventurous skiing but not too bulky

Trousers are lightweight yet warm and waterproof

Outfit is practical and comfortable – just what a good skier needs

Goggles are the best non-steam on the market

### what it says about you

"I know what I am doing, I'm not a flashy airhead. My style is in my impeccable slalom so I'm going to look great on the slopes anyway, whatever I wear."

### on the slopes/ beginner

✗ Wearing jeans to ski in might save money, but you'll be put off for life after a few hours of skiing in soggy clothes

However long your jacket is, it won't be enough to keep the snow out when worn with ordinary trousers

A fun hat might make it easier for the instructor to find you, but you'll be the laughingstock of the slopes

### what it says about you

"I'm a party girl who probably won't bother turning up to classes because I'll be too hung over. When I do, I'll screw around, which will be funny at first but then get on everybody's nerves."

## on the slopes/ beginner

An all-in-one is the most comfortable thing to wear when you're learning to ski. No snow will get inside, you'll be warm all day. If you get too hot, you can control the input of cool air through the zipper down your front

Dark color means you'll be seen even in a blizzard

Hat is warm and traditional

### what it says about you

"I really want to learn to ski. I've borrowed this suit because I want to find out if I like whizzing headfirst down a mountain before I lash out the cash for my own outfit."

## on the slopes/poser

✗ A poser wants to look like how she thinks a professional might look if they had time to think about it

Once you know how to ski, the all-in-one, in a pastel tone, should be sent to the second-hand shop

Fabric is billowy and makes the butt twice the size

**what it says about you**

"I'm only here to be seen. The closest I'll get to any ice is in my mineral water."

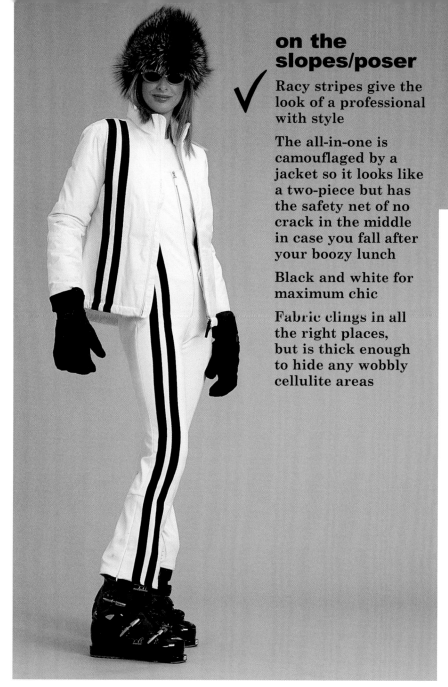

## on the slopes/poser

✓ Racy stripes give the look of a professional with style

The all-in-one is camouflaged by a jacket so it looks like a two-piece but has the safety net of no crack in the middle in case you fall after your boozy lunch

Black and white for maximum chic

Fabric clings in all the right places, but is thick enough to hide any wobbly cellulite areas

### what it says about you

"I'm a fair-weather skier and proud of it. Take me as I am and you'll love or hate me. If it's the latter, you won't spoil my holiday."

## après ski

**X** The evening will always be below freezing so even a fur vest cannot be worn with nothing underneath

You're climbing mountains not the New York social scene

Overdone hair should be left in the metropolis

### what it says about you

"I'm more used to country houses than ski resorts. I thought I should wear something warm... then I changed my mind."

## après ski

✓ Don't bother with fancy jewelry as it will always be too much

Winter white is the ultimate in mountain chic

Wearing hair down will prevent frostbitten ears

### what it says about you

"I've had a great day on the slopes and I'm going to have an equally good evening. I know how to combine looking gorgeous with being warm and comfortable."

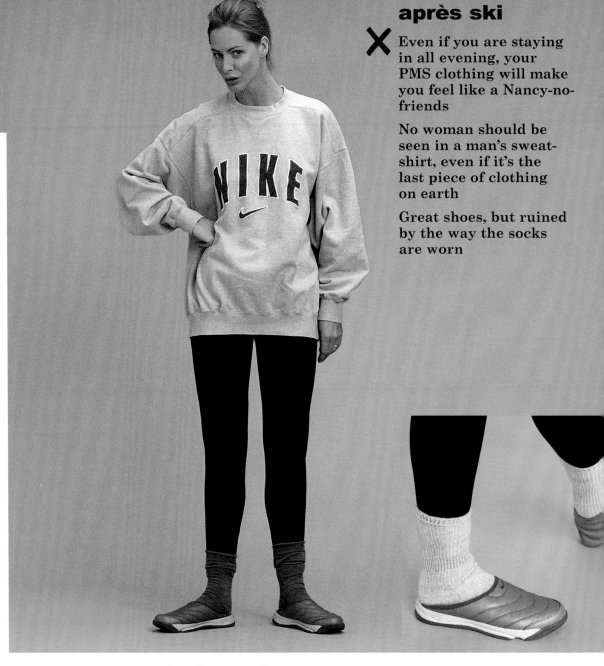

## après ski

**X** Even if you are staying in all evening, your PMS clothing will make you feel like a Nancy-no-friends

No woman should be seen in a man's sweatshirt, even if it's the last piece of clothing on earth

Great shoes, but ruined by the way the socks are worn

### what it says about you

"I don't want to appeal to anyone. I'm not worthy of human contact and should be kept in a cupboard under the stairs."

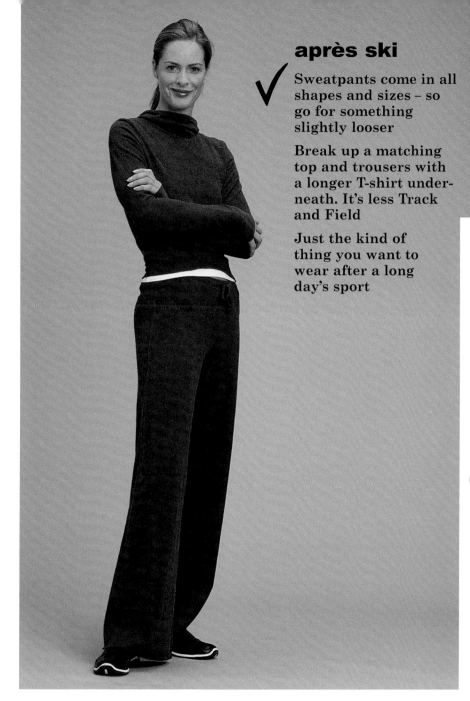

## après ski

✓ Sweatpants come in all shapes and sizes – so go for something slightly looser

Break up a matching top and trousers with a longer T-shirt underneath. It's less Track and Field

Just the kind of thing you want to wear after a long day's sport

**what it says about you**

"Boy, I've had a truly tiring day off-piste. The snow was fabulous. This is all bullshit, but no one will know because my slick gear speaks 'athlete.'"

## après ski

✗ Wearing the trendiest look at a mountain resort will make you stand out as beginner

Very high heels turn roads into ice rinks

A mini with no tights looks simply ridiculous in such cold weather

### what it says about you

"I've never been skiing before and I'm too stupid to realize that what I wear in my local club back home is neither practical nor appropriate."

## après ski

✓ Jeans are the best
basic to build on

Sweaters can look very
sexy if they are fitted
and plunging

Long scarf keeps neck
warm and looks cool

Boots are practically
low but not too clumpy

### what it says about you

"Come on, let's get a few schnapps in us, go out
dancing and be up in time to take in a full day's skiing.
Yes, I'm a girl who knows how to balance major fun
with serious skiing."

# winter holiday/on the slopes/apres ski

| | $ | $$ | $$$ |
|---|---|---|---|
| **professional** | Patagonia, Gap, J. Crew, Lands' End, Columbia Sportswear Company, Eddie Bauer<br>**Accessories**<br>Gap, Banana Republic, J. Crew, Lands' End | Billabong, Rip Curl, O'Neills, Quiksilver, The North Face, Seven for All Mankind, Juicy Couture, Joseph, Burton<br>**Accessories**<br>The North Face, Quiksilver, Billabong, Kors by Michael Kors, Ugg, Joseph | Prada, Gucci, Ralph Lauren, Temperley, Plein Sud, Dries van Noten<br>**Accessories**<br>Michael Kors, Sigerson Morrison |
| **beginner** | Target, Gap, H & M, Macy's, Burlington Coat Factory, Target<br>**Accessories**<br>Target, Gap, Patagonia | Oakley, Puma, Nike, Calvin Klein Underwear, Wolford, Snow + Rock<br>**Accessories**<br>Puma, Nike, Ugg | Helly Hansen, Nuala, Prada Sport, La Perla, Hogan, Tod's<br>**Accessories**<br>Hogan, Tod's, Burberry |
| **poser** | Zara, H & M, Urban Outfitters, Patagonia, Banana Republic, Abercrombie & Fitch<br>**Accessories**<br>Zara, Banana Republic, Claire's | Snow + Rock, Polo, French Connection, Tommy Hilfiger, Joseph<br>**Accessories**<br>Oakley, Ugg, Kors by Michael Kors, Joseph | Ralph Lauren, Escada, Chanel, Temperley, Prada, Alexander McQueen, Vivienne Westwood, Donna Karan, Calvin Klein<br>**Accessories**<br>Erickson Beamon, Graff |

**where to shop**

# winter holiday

- If your sunglasses are too big, the suntan marks after a hard day's skiing will drive you crazy. Take smaller, thirties-style, wraparound ones that still give protection, yet allow for a natural mark-free tan

- Always cut your toenails before getting fitted for ski boots, otherwise the amount of pressure you put on them when skiing could make your toenails fall off

- When skiing in very cold conditions, it's far better to add more layers than wear heavy clothes. Layers provide more places for your body heat to be trapped

- If you suffer from bad circulation, don't forget to pack hand and foot warmers – found in any skiing or shooting shop

- A foot massage in the evening will stimulate tired muscles and prepare you for your ski boots the following day. Weleda does a fantastic arnica version you can also put in the bath

- If you are quite unfit or relatively new to skiing, take arnica in preparation for falls and tired muscles

- Apply sun protection liberally. Winter sun and wind can burn, even in January

- Take Visine on the slopes for tired, hung-over or wind-damaged eyes

- Always have some tissues with you as so many rest rooms don't have any

tips

**partying** Enjoying a party is as much about feeling smug in the knowledge that you look divine as it is about who you hang with and how much alcohol is consumed. The key is to forget the kind of people that are going to be there and focus on the type of event it is you've been invited to. Stick to what suits your shape and consider how smart you want to be. If you want to stand out from the crowd, it's easier to do so by over-dressing a bit. This doesn't mean raiding the kids dressing-up box. We are thinking more about glamour than fancy dress. Just because a bash is in the garden with food cooked on an open fire doesn't mean you have to forego style. Play it down with jeans, then ramp up the sex appeal. A subtle cleavage or peek of midriff will be enough to make you the center of attention. Looking as though you were born at a film premiere or a black tie ball is what creates charisma. Trying too hard, being predictable ("she always looks like that") or not bothering at all are easy mistakes to make and a turn-off. Focus on your physical strengths, be true to your individuality and remember subdued sexuality is better than overexposure. You'll look great. Have a ball!

# partying

**9**

## winter

✗ If you buy only one evening dress a year, choosing velvet will only allow a winter outing

A feather boa should be kept for the cast of *Moulin Rouge* or fancy dress

Long black satin gloves show that you either have a problem with nail biting or live in another era

### what it says about you

"I'm a loud show-off, who will blast your eardrums and empty the dance floor with my over-the-top antics."

# winter

✓ Satin is one of the most luxurious – yet sexy – fabrics to wear in the evening

The jacket brings glamour to a simple dress and makes an outfit more adaptable. If you arrive and find everyone is more casual – whisk it off

The shoes are elegant, yet unobtrusive. With an evening dress shoes should be seen but not heard

## what it says about you

"I don't need to show off my boobs and acres of leg to look sexy. I know that an understated, clinging number can be much more intriguing."

# winter

**✗** Being too dressed up at your own dinner party can intimidate the guests and make them feel they should do the kitchen work

Tottering heels at home look like you are about to leave any minute

**partying casual**

### what it says about you
"I'm not really too at ease with all this entertaining and this is probably going to be a difficult evening for me as well as you."

# winter

✓ A gorgeous skirt with a simple top looks elegant yet informal

Shoes can be kitten, flat or kicked off

Long skirt or loose trousers are relaxed and lounge-proof

## what it says about you

"I know how to be comfortable as well as look good so I can relax and enjoy myself with friends without worrying about whether I'm creasing my clothes."

## winter

**✕** Urban outfits should be unfussy – not too many frills and flounces

Black and white will encourage guests to keep asking you for a drink

If you use hot rollers in your hair, remember to brush out afterward

### what it says about you

"I've overdone my outfit to make up for my lack of charm and conversation. I'll probably need to rush to the ladies' every five minutes to check my frills and curls."

## winter

✓ You can't go wrong with black if it suits you and if it doesn't, keep it as far from your face as possible

Simple chic speaks volumes in terms of style

Make sure heels aren't too high for a standing event

### what it says about you

"My clothes are understated, yet elegant and I'm confident that I look great without being overly formal. Nothing fussy – just perfection."

## summer

✗ Over-the-top sparkle
doesn't compensate for
a short length if the
invitation is for long

Be careful with sequins as
they can be very enlarging

They can also be very tacky
if displayed en masse

**partying smart**

### what it says about you

"Don't have a long frock so maybe if I wear something
tight and showy everyone will be too busy admiring
my bum to notice that I'm not dressed right."

## summer

✓ Long is always elegant
and flattering

A simple dress is
easy to adapt to the
smartness of the
occasion

Dress it up and down
with accessories

**what it says about you**

"I don't need to pile on the glitz. My dress may be plain
but the shawl is a showstopper and I know how to carry
it off with style."

## summer

✗ White at a barbecue may be very Great Gatsby but it's totally impractical

High heels will sink into the grass

If you're sitting on the ground, picnic style, in a skirt, your undies will be on show

Hat is a little too much

### what it says about you

"I don't really like being outdoors and I'm frightened of getting mud on my shoes so I don't think I'll enjoy myself or stay very long."

## summer

✓ Jeans allow for rough-and-ready outdoor treatment

Top could be the only thing seen if there's a crowd of guests so make sure it's pretty

Comfort is as much a factor as style

### what it says about you

"I know how to look sexy but I'll still pitch in and do my turn at the barbecue. And if get ketchup on my jeans... what the hell!"

## summer

✗ Don't be fooled into thinking short equals sexy

Childish hairstyles are great...on children

Don't wear a trend unless it suits you – you'll be the laughing-stock of the party rather than the envy of fellow guests

### what it says about you

"I'm just a girlie at heart so if I wear girlie clothes no one will notice that I've, well... gotten a little older."

## summer

✓ If there isn't a trendy look you feel comfortable with, choose the colors and fabrics that are in

It's easier to be trendy and look good with separates

Separates also get more use, as they can be worn with other things

### what it says about you

"I always manage to look up to the minute – but in my own individual way. Well-chosen separates are the backbone of my wardrobe."

## partying/winter

| | $ | $$ | $$$ |
|---|---|---|---|
| **smart** | Zara, Banana Republic, J. Crew, Express<br>**Accessories**<br>Claire's, Express, Banana Republic | Nicole Miller, DKNY, Adrienne Vittadini, BCBG, Laundry<br>**Accessories**<br>Nicole Miller, BCBG, Agatha, Kenneth Cole | Temperley, Ralph Lauren, Calvin Klein, Alberta Ferretti, Gucci, Prada, Vivienne Westwood, Jean Paul Gautier, Armani, John Galliano, Alexander McQueen, Valentino<br>**Accessories**<br>Gucci, Prada, Jimmo Choo, Manolo Blahnik |
| **casual** | Zara, Target, H & M, Express, Gap Body<br>**Accessories**<br>Claire's , Target, Swatch | French Connection, Michael Stars, Juicy Couture, Diesel, Seven for All Mankind<br>**Accessories**<br>Donald Pliner, Puma, Diesel | Marni, Temperley, Chloé, Ghost<br>**Accessories**<br>Marni, Sigerson Morrison, Prada |
| **trendy** | Urban Outfitters, Zara, H & M, Express<br>**Accessories**<br>Zara, H & M, Girlshop | BCBG, Development, French Connection, Marc by Marc Jacobs, DKNY, A. B. S.<br>**Accessories**<br>Agatha, Christian Dior, Marc by Marc Jacobs | Prada, Dolce & Gabbana, Roberto Cavalli, Temperley, Blumarine, Chloé, Marc Jacobs<br>**Accessories**<br>Sigerson Morrison, Jimmy Choo, Christian Louboutin, Erickson Beamon |

## partying/summer

| | $ | $$ | $$$ |
|---|---|---|---|
| **smart** | H & M, Club Monaco, Banana Republic, J. Crew<br>**Accessories**<br>Zara, Banana Republic, H & M | Nicole Miller, Theory, BCBG, Betsey Johnson, Theory<br>**Accessories**<br>Agatha, BCBG, Kenneth Cole | Tuleh, Temperley, Alberta Ferretti, Gucci, Prada, Armani, Vivienne Westwood, John Galliano<br>**Accessories**<br>Gucci, Prada, Jimmy Choo, Manolo Blahnik, Valentino, Erickson Beamon |
| **casual** | Gap, H & M, Target, Zara, Banana Republic<br>**Accessories**<br>Target, Zara, Express | French Connection, Diesel, Lacoste, Seven for All Mankind, Anthropologie, Betsey Johnson<br>**Accessories**<br>Anthropologie, Puma, Diesel | Cacharel, Marni, Temperley, Paper Denim & Cloth, Marc Jacobs<br>**Accessories**<br>Sigerson Morrison, Pippa Small, Erickson Beamon |
| **trendy** | H & M, Urban Outfitters, Zara, Girlshop, Express<br>**Accessories**<br>H & M, Zara, Express | Olive and Bette's, French Connection, Michael Stars, Marc by Marc Jacobs, DKNY, Joseph<br>**Accessories**<br>Agatha, DKNY, Olive and Bette's, Scoop NYC, Me & Ro | Narciso Rodriguez, Louis Vuitton, Missoni, Marc Jacobs, Fendi, Etro, Blumarine, Temperley<br>**Accessories**<br>Christian Louboutin, Sigerson Morrison, Louis Vuitton, Pippa Small |

# partying

- Cut down makeup to fit into an evening bag and yet retain all your requirements. For instance, sharpen down pencils – it's not a waste, you'll always lose them before they're ground down – and put loose powder in a small MAC powder container

- If you are in for a long night, use a makeup primer under your foundation. Check out Laura Mercier, Nars, Vincent Longo.

- Don't take such a big bag that you end up having to dance around it all evening

- Think whether your shoes will carry you through the night

- If you're wearing a smart evening outfit, don't ruin it with a daytime watch

- Are you likely to get your period? Take Tampax

- If you're planning on getting smashed, think about heel height – and falling over

- Eat a few almonds to line an empty stomach if you're going to drink a lot before dinner

- Mints for the sexy kiss

- If you're going to a big event in winter, consider taking a shawl instead of a heavy coat so you can avoid the coat check line in and out

- Do make sure you've got enough money for a cab if things don't go as planned

tips

**underwear** Are you aware that three-quarters of you are wearing the wrong-sized bra? Look down. Do your boobs give off a vibe of wanting to escape? Are they sneaking over the top of the lace? Turn around. Do you see your bra straps digging furrows in your back and is there a feeling of a restraining order being imposed upon your udders? Keeping your eyes downcast, do you see the outline of pretty lace through your T-shirt? Or worse, has the sexy black lace turned dirty gray when covered with a pale top? Hmm. Now, it's time to get off your arse to check the state of your butt in a full-length mirror. How many cheeks do you see? Two or four? Would an onlooker be aware that you prefer briefs to g-strings? And talking of g-strings, when you bend over to pick up a toy or a boy, does a rather nasty worn-out Y appear above the waistband? Swivel to the side. How does your tummy look? Ready to deliver a litter or dough-like and bloated? If any of the above applies to your clothed anatomy, waste no time in correcting the problem. What's the point of pouring time and effort into cool looks when your underwear is a mess?

# underwear

10

## problem/flabby tummy

**X** Ask all but flat-stomached freaks what they detest most about their bodies and the unanimous cry will be "my bloody tummy." A flabby tummy is the most hated defect among women

### what's the problem?

"The tummy is an impossible area to get back into shape after having kids and the bane of those who like a carb fix from time to time. If you're not going to resort to surgery, then we advise the use of radical underwear."

## solution

✓ Power Panties create smooth, sleek lines enabling you to wear figure-hugging clothes that you might have banned from your life for years

### what to do

"Wear Power Panties. They may not eradicate tummy bulges altogether, but they will make soft flesh firm and wobble-free and give the tum an instant iron-out."

## problem/ visible g-string

**X** You don't think of the impact your thong might have when you bend or crouch down or when your jeans slither down your hips

### what's the problem?

"Visible thongs are really only a problem for those partial to hipster trousers and low-slung waistbands. But we are here to tell you a crusty, worn-out g-string is not a pretty sight."

## solution

✓ If you're going to flash your knickers, make sure they're worth looking at rather than a barren triangle of grubby nylon

### what to do

"Luckily there are people who care enough about our butts. These Guardians of the Rear have come up with prettily decorated thongs that flash sequined butterflies and the like."

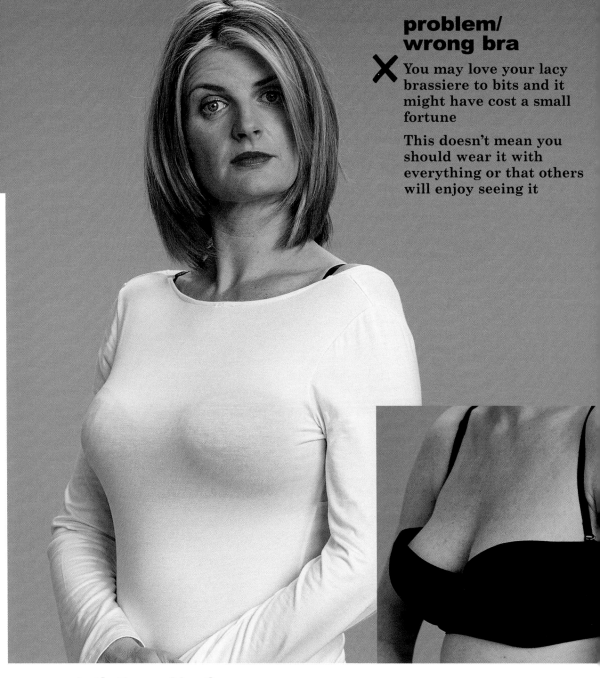

## problem/ wrong bra

✗ You may love your lacy brassiere to bits and it might have cost a small fortune

This doesn't mean you should wear it with everything or that others will enjoy seeing it

### what's the problem?
"The wrong bra can rough up your pale or smooth-fitting tops. It is such a shame to ruin the possibility of a smart clean line with a black or over-adorned bra."

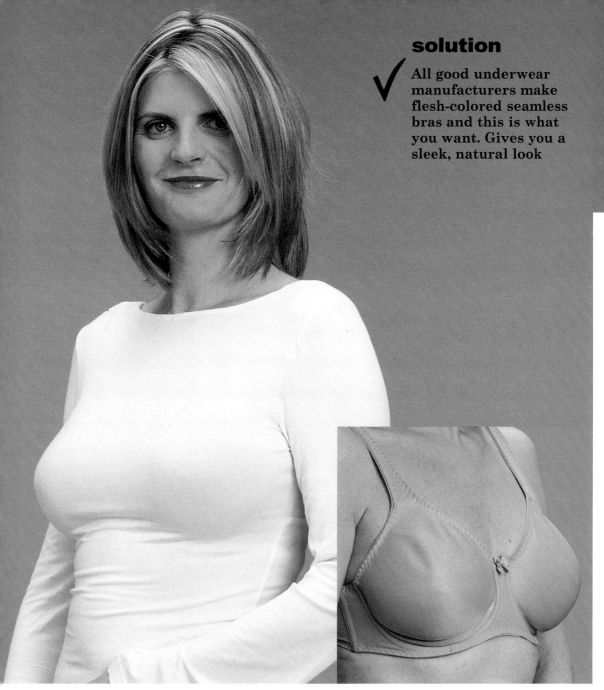

## solution

✓ All good underwear manufacturers make flesh-colored seamless bras and this is what you want. Gives you a sleek, natural look

## what to do

"Be sure to have your bra properly fitted so that your boobs don't spill out the top and the straps don't dig into the shoulders or back."

## underwear

| | $ | $$ | $$$ |
|---|---|---|---|
| **sexy** | H & M, Victoria's Secret, Le Mystère, Pretty Polly | Cosabella, Calvin Klein Underwear, Fantasie of England, Eberjey | La Perla, Agent Provocateur, Donna Karan Malizia |
| **athletic** | Maidenform, Gap Body, H & M | Nike, DKNY, Calvin Klein Underwear | La Perla Sport Spanx Power Panties, Wolford |

## underwear

- Always make sure you have your bits done

- If you are wearing tight trousers don't wear bikini panties – they will cut your butt cheeks in half

- Bridget Jones knickers won't get you laid, but magic underpants will keep your tummy in

- Breasts can change size. Keep getting your size checked and get a bra that fits

- If you are flat-chested but find yourself in need of a flesh-colored bra to wear under a skimpy outfit, cut up a pair of flesh-colored tights above the gusset, make it into a bandeau and slip it on like a bra

- If you're wearing a calf-length skirt, don't take the risk of wearing knee-highs – they will be seen

- If you're going out in the evening and intend to have bare legs, don't wear knee-highs during the day as the marks won't have gone

- If you have to wear nylons with sandals make sure the toe is seamless

- If you're going to wear a backless dress in the evening, be aware of the tightness of your bra during the day. Any marks will show later

- Don't machine-wash an underwire bra because the plastic bobble at the end will melt, allowing the sharp wiring to poke through the fabric

A. B. S.—www.absstyle.com

Abercrombie & Fitch—
www.abercrombie.com

Adidas—www.adidas.com

Adrienne Vittadini—
www.adriennevittadini.com

Agatha—800-AGATHA7
www.agatha.co.jp

Agent Provocateur—
www.agentprovocateur.com

Agnès b.—www.agnesb.com

Alberta Ferretti—
www.albertaferretti.com

Alexander McQueen—
www.alexandermcqueen.net

Alice + Olivia—www.aliceandolivia.com

Allegra Hicks—www.allegrahicks.com

Ann-Louise Roswald—
www.annlouiseroswald.com

Ann Taylor—www.anntaylor.com

Anthropologie—800-543-1039
www.anthropologie.com

Anya Hindmarch—
www.anyahindmarch.com

Armani—www.giorgioarmani.com

Balenciago—www.balenciago.com

Banana Republic—888-BRSTYLE
www.bananarepublic.com

BCBG—888-636-BCBG
www.bcbg.com

Benetton—www.benetton.com

Betsey Johnson—877-464-3293
www.betseyjohnson.com

Billabong—www.billabong.com

Birkenstock—
www.birkenstock.com

Blue Cult—www.blaec.com

Blumarine—www.blumarine.com

Boss Woman—www.bosswoman.com

Bottega Veneta—www.bottegaveneta.com

Brooks Brothers—
www.brooksbrothers.com

Bulgari—www.bulgari.com

Burberry—www.burberry.com

Burlington Coat Factory—
www.burlingtoncoatfactory.com

Cacharel—www.cacharel.com

Calvin Klein—www.saksfifthavenue.com

Calvin Klein Underwear—
www.barenecessities.com

Cartier—www.cartier.com

Catherine Malandrino—
www.catherinemalandrino.com

Celine—www.celine.com

Chanel—www.chanel.com

Charles Jourdan—
www.charles-jourdan.com

Chloé—www.chloe.com

Christian Dior—www.dior.com

Christian Louboutin—
www.net-a-porter.com

Claire's—www.claires.com

Club Monaco—www.clubmonaco.com

Columbia Sportswear Company—
www.columbia.com

Comme des Garcons—
www.comme-des-garcons.silkrunway.com

Cosabella—www.cosabella.com

Costume National—
www.costumenational.com

Cynthia Rowley—
www.cynthiarowley.com

Development—www.blaec.com

Diane von Furstenberg—www.dvf.com

Diesel—212-755-9200
www.diesel.com

DKNY—www.dkny.com

Dolce & Gabbana—
www.dolcegabbana.com

Donald Pliner—www.donaldjpliner.com

Donna Karan—www.donnakaran.com

Dooney & Bourke—www.dooney.com

Dosa—www.dosainc.com

Dries van Noten—www.driesvannoten.be

Earl Jean—www.earljean.com

Eberjey—www.eberjey.com

Eddie Bauer—www.eddiebauer.com

Emanuel Ungaro—
www.emanuelungaro.com

Emilio Pucci—www.pucci.com

Erickson Beamon—www.net-a-porter.com

Escada—www.escada.com

Escada Sport—www.escada.com

Etro—www.etro.it

Express—www.expressfashion.com

Fantasie of England—
www.barenecessities.com

Fendi—www.fendi.com

French Connection—
www.frenchconnection.com

Furla—www.furla.com

Gap—800-GAP-STYLE
www.gap.com

Gap Body—www.gap.com

Girlshop—www.girlshop.com

Givenchy—www.givenchy.com

Ghost—www.ghost.co.uk

Graff—www.graffdiamonds.com

Gucci—www.gucci.com
www.neimanmarcus.com

Gucci Cruise—www.gucci.com

Guess—www.guess.com

H & M—www.hm.com

Helly Hansen—www.hellyhansen.com

Helmut Lang—www.helmutlang.com

Hermès—www.hermes.com

Hervé Chapelier—
www.herve-chapelier.com

Hogan—www.designer-apparel-
store.com/Hogan-Designer-Apparel-1.asp

Hollywood Trading Company—
www.blaec.com

Hollywould—www.ilovehollywould.com

Isaac Mizrahi for Target—
www.Target.com

Jamin Puech—
www.jamin-puech.silkrunway.com

J. Crew—800-932-0043
www.jcrew.com

Jill Stuart—www.jillstuart.com

Jimmy Choo—www.jimmychoo.com

John Galliano—www.johngalliano.com

Jean Paul Gautier—
   www.jeanpaul-gautier.com
John Smedley—www.john-smedley.com
Jones New York—www.jonesnewyork.com
Joseph—www.designer-clothing-
   search.co.uk/Joseph
Juicy Couture—www.juicycouture.com

Katayone Adeli—www.bluefly.com
   www.net-a-porter.com
Kate Spade—www.katespade.com
Kenneth Cole—800-KEN-COLE
   www.kennethcole.com
Kors Michael Kors—www.shopbop.com

Lacoste—www.lacoste.com
Lands' End—
   www.landsend.com
La Perla—www.laperla.com
Laundry—
   www.edressme.com/laundry.html
Le Mystère—www.lemystere.com
Longchamp—www.longchamp.com
Louis Vuitton—www.vuitton.com

Macy's—www.macys.com
Magic Knickers—www.practicalprincess.net
Maharishi—www.net-a-porter.com
Maidenform—www.maidenform.com
Malizia—www.barenecessities.com
Manolo Blahnik—www.neimanmarcus.com
Marc Jacobs—www.marcjacobs.com
   www.eluxury.com
Marc by Marc Jacobs—
   www.marcjacobs.com
   www.eluxury.com
   www.net-a-porter.com
Marni—www.net-a-porter.com
Max Mara—www.saksfifthavenue.com
Me & Ro—www.meandrojewelry.com
Michael Kors—www.michaelkors.com
Michael Stars—www.michaelstars.com
Missoni—www.missoni.com
Miss Sixty—www.misssixty.com
   www.shopbop.com
Miu Miu—www.miumiu.com
Moschino—www.moschino.com

Muji—www.mujionline.com

Nanette Lepore—www.nanettelepore.com
Narciso Rodriguez—www.net-a-porter.com
Nicole Farhi—www.nicolefarhi.com
Nicole Miller—www.nicolemiller.com
Nike—www.nike.com
Nine West—www.ninewest.com
The North Face—www.northface.com
Nuala—888-565-7862
   www.nuala.puma.com

Oakley—www.oakley.com
Olive and Bette's—
   www.oliveandbettes.com
O'Neills—www.oneills.com
Only Hearts—www.blaec.com

Paper Denim & Cloth—www.blaec.com
Patagonia—www.patagonia.com
Patch NYC—www.patchnyc.com
Paul & Joe—www.paul-joe-beaute.com
Paul Smith—www.paulsmith.co.uk
Petit Bateau—212-988-8884
   www.petit-bateau.com
Philip Treacy—www.philiptreacy.co.uk
Pippa Small—www.pippasmall.com
Polo—www.polo.com
Prada—www.prada.com
   www.neimanmarcus.com
Prada Sport—www.prada.com
Pretty Polly—www.mytights.com
Puma—www.puma.com
Punk Royal—www.blaec.com

Quiksilver—www.PacSun.com

Ralph Lauren—www.polo.com
Rebecca Taylor—www.rebeccataylor.com
Rip Curl—www.ripcurl.com
Rite Aid—www.riteaid.com
Roberto Cavalli—www.robertocavalli.com
Roberto Coin—www.robertocoin.com
   www.neimanmarcus.com

Sara James—www.sarajames.biz
Scoop NYC—www.scoopnyc.com

Searle—www.searlenyc.com
Seven for All Mankind—www.shopbop.com
Sigerson Morrison—
   www.sigersonmorrison.com
Snow + Rock—www.snowandrock.com
Solange Azagury-Partridge—
   www.solangeazagurypartridge.com
Spanx—www.spanx.com
Stella McCartney—
   www.stellamccartney.com
Steve Madden—www.stevemadden.com
Swarovski—www.swarovski.com
Swatch—www.swatch.com

Target—www.target.com
Temperley—www.net-a-porter.com
The Container Store—
   www.containerstore.com
Theory—www.theory.com
   www.shopbop.com
Thomas Pink—www.thomaspink.com
Three Dots—www.tee-zone.com
Tocca—www.tocca.com
Tod's—www.tods.com
Tommy Hilfiger—www.tommy.com
Tuleh—www.designerexposure.com

Ugg—www.uggs.com
Uncommongoods.com—
   www.uncommongoods.com
Urban Outfitters—www.urbanoutfitters.com

Valentino—www.valentino.it
Van Cleef and Arpels—www.vancleef.com
Vanessa Bruno—www.net-a-porter.com
Velvet—www.shopbop.com
Versace—www.versace.com
Victoria's Secret—www.victoriassecret.com
Vivienne Westwood—
   www.viviennewestwood.com

White—www.blaec.com
Wolford—www.wolford.com

Yves Saint Laurent—www.ysl.com

Zara—www.zara.com

# JUDITH BLACKLOCK
# FLOWER SCHOOL

## KNIGHTSBRIDGE

*Courses in flower arranging and floristry, lasting from a half day to two weeks.*

**For further information contact**

### *The Judith Blacklock Flower School, Knightsbridge.*
Telephone **+44 (0) 20 7235 6235**, Fax **+44 (0) 20 7235 6335**,
E-mail: **school@judithblacklock.com**   Website: **www.judithblacklock.com**

# the A-Z of teach yourself

## teach yourself®

Afrikaans
Access 2002
Accounting, Basic
Alexander Technique
Algebra
Arabic
Arabic Script, Beginner's
Aromatherapy
Astronomy
Bach Flower Remedies
Beginner's Turkish
Bengali
Better Chess
Better Handwriting
Biology
Body Language
Book Keeping
Book Keeping & Accounting
Brazilian Portuguese
Bridge
Buddhism
Bulgarian
Business Studies
C++
Calculus
Cantonese
Card Games
Catalan
Chess
Chi Kung
Chinese
Chinese Script, Beginner's
Chinese, Beginner's
Christianity
Classical Music
Copywriting
Counselling
Creative Writing
Crime Fiction
Croatian
Crystal Healing
Czech
Danish
Desktop Publishing
Digital Photography
Digital Video & PC Editing
Drawing
Dream Interpretation
Dutch
Dutch Dictionary
Dutch Grammar
Dutch, Beginner's
Eastern Philosophy
ECDL
E-Commerce
Electronics

Engish Grammar as a Foreign Language
English as a Foreign Language
English for International Business
English Grammar
English Language, Life & Culture
English Verbs
English Vocabulary
English, American, as a Foreign Language
English, Correct
English, Instant, for German Speakers
English, Instant, for Italian Speakers
English, Instant, for Spanish Speakers
English, Teaching One to One
Ethics
Excel 2002
Feng Shui
Film Making
Film Studies
Finance for nn-Financial Managers
Finnish
Flexible Working
Flower Arranging
French
French Grammar
French Grammar, Quick Fix
French Language, Life & Culture
French Starter Kit
French Verbs
French Vocabulary
French, Beginner's
French, Instant
Gaelic
Gaelic Dictionary
Genetics
Geology
German
German Grammar
German Grammar, Quick Fix
German Language, Life & Culture
German Verbs
German Vocabulary
German, Beginner's
German, Instant
Go
Golf
Greek
Greek Script, Beginner's
Greek, Ancient
Greek, Beginner's
Greek, Instant
Greek, New Testament
Guitar
Gulf Arabic
Hand Reflexology
Hebrew, Biblical
Herbal Medicine
Hieroglyphics
Hindi
Hindi Script, Beginner's
Hindi, Beginner's
Hinduism
How to Win at Horse Racing
How to Win at Poker
HTML Publishing on the WWW
Human Anatomy & Physiology
Hungarian
Icelandic
Indian Head Massage
Indonesian
Internet, The
Irish

Islam
Italian
Italian Grammar
Italian Grammar, Quick Fix
Italian Language, Life & Culture
Italian Verbs
Italian Vocabulary
Italian, Beginner's
Italian, Instant
Japanese
Japanese Language, Life & Culture
Japanese Script, Beginner's
Japanese, Beginner's
Japanese, Instant
Java
Jewellery Making
Judaism
Korean
Latin
Latin American Spanish
Latin Dictionary
Latin Grammar
Latin, Beginner's
Letter Writing Skills
Linguistics
Mah Jong
Managing Stress
Marketing
Massage
Mathematics
Mathematics, Basic
Media Studies
Meditation
Mosaics
Music Theory
Needlecraft
Negotiating
Nepali
Norwegian
Origami
Panjabi
Persian, Modern
Philosophy
Philosophy of Mind
Philosophy of Religion
Philosophy of Science
Photography
Photoshop
Physics
Piano
Planets
Planning Your Wedding
Polish
Politics
Portuguese
Portuguese Grammar
Portuguese Language Life & Culture
Portuguese, Beginner's
Portuguese, Brazilian
Portuguese, Instant
Postmodernism
Pottery
Powerpoint 2002
Presenting for Professionals
Project Management
Psychology
Psychology, Applied
Quark Xpress
Quilting
Recruitment
Reflexology

Reiki
Relaxation
Retaining Staff
Romanian
Russian
Russian Grammar
Russian Language Life & Culture
Russian Script, Beginner's
Russian, Beginner's
Russian, Instant
Sanskrit
Screenwriting
Serbian
Setting up a Small Business
Shorthand, Pitman 2000
Sikhism
Spanish
Spanish Grammar
Spanish Grammar, Quick Fix
Spanish Language, Life & Culture
Spanish Starter Kit
Spanish Verbs
Spanish Vocabulary
Spanish, Beginner's
Spanish, Instant
Speaking on Special Occasions
Speed Reading
Statistical Research
Statistics
Swahili
Swahili
Swahili Dictionary
Swedish
Tagalog
Tai Chi
Tantric Sex
Teaching English as Foreign Language
Teams and Team-Working
Thai
Time Management
Tracing your Family History
Travel Writing
Trigonometry
Turkish
Typing
Ukrainian
Urdu
Urdu Script, Beginner's
Vietnamese
Volcanoes
Watercolour Painting
Weight Control through Diet and Exercise
Welsh
Welsh
Welsh Dictionary
Welsh Language Life & Culture
Wills and Probate
Wine Tasting
Winning at Job Interviews
Word 2002
World Faiths
Writing a Novel
Writing for Children
Writing Poetry
Xhosa
Yoga
Zen
Zulu

## The plant material

The parallel horizontal placements are best created with natural plant material such as *Eucalyptus* bark, straight-sided pieces of *Cornus*, *Equisetum*, long cinnamon sticks, pampas grass (*Cortaderia*) or *Phormium* leaves. Branches of blossom, *Angelica* stems, bundled stripped willow and slivers of driftwood can also be used.

Bold flowers provide contrast and should complement the basic structure without changing the style. *Gerbera*, bloom chrysanthemums, *Anthurium*, calla (*Zantedeschia*) all work well.

Alternatively, you could use fruit or vegetables such as lemons, sharon fruit, ornamental cabbages or even halves of red cabbage in larger designs. You could also include non plant material such as metal pieces and plexi glass.

## The design

- Different kinds of flowers and foliage can be used together. Delicate flowers such as jasmine can be used with bolder plant material.
- Bold forms tend to dominate.
- Moss can be used to camouflage the foam and give added texture.
- Space and rhythm can be added by introducing repeating looped linear leaves.

## Creating the design

1. Place the foam in the container so that it is about one third of the height of the container once in position.
2. Take the linear foliage or bark and build up your layers. Create depth by building out at varying lengths and at varying depths. If possible run a piece the full length of the design. To keep these in place wrap a strong wire round the centre of the bark or stem and insert the free ends in the foam or use a bradawl to make holes through the plant material and loop your wire through and into the foam. Alternatively if a length is heavy hot glue kebab sticks to the wood at right angles to insert into the foam.
3. Cover the foam with moss and/or leaves. Build up rhythm by overlapping leaves. You could use well-conditioned leaves of *Parthenocissus tricuspicata*, *Hedera*, *Ribes*, *Fatsia* or *Fatshedera*, manipulated *Cordyline* leaves or looped bear grass to give added depth.
4. Add bold flowers such as *Anthurium*, *Gerbera*, bloom chrysanthemums and other items to add interest.

- Previous page: The design of the shell-shaped vase is repeated in the form of the wavy leaves of the *Brahea*. Its glossy texture contrasts with the dull and rough pieces of black kelp. A further contrast is evident between the spathes of *Pandanus utilis* and the cork bark which has been bleached so that the colour of the two elements is similar but the texture totally different. Other material used is *Begonia rex*, *Crassula falcata*, *Crassula hyb.*, *Furcraea foetida*, *Hedychium gardnerianum*, *Kniphofia* hyb. and *Quercus suber*.

# Inspiration

■ The flowing, undulating stems of the turban flowers (*Ranunculas*) and tulips give a rhythmic arrangement in a simple glass container. The smooth-textured green leaves of the tulips add substance and complement the round forms of the flowers.

**flower arranging**

■ Anemones are happiest with their stems in water. This topiary has been created by inserting a florist's extension cone in foam and tightly packing green garden sticks around the cone to give a decorative finish.

■ Split, dried oranges provide the focus for this simple arrangement of *Azigozanthus* (kangaroo paw), *Asclepias*, *Photinia* and *Hypericum* in a straight-sided brown pot.

**flower arranging**

■ Chicken wire covers a simple basket container through which twigs have been inserted. Hypericum, huckleberry, waxflower, red Cordyline leaves and stunning Oriental lilies fill the container. Twigs of pussy willow link with the container and give overall unity to the design.

■ *Gypsophila* always looks good on its own, creating a cloud of colour and texture. The smooth stones at the base complement the flowers, subtly yet dramatically. Further contrast is given by the terracotta container and palisade of brown stems.

# Taking it further

## Flower Arranging Worldwide

The World Association of Flower Arrangers (WAFA) was founded in 1981. Up-to-date information may be obtained from the National Association of Flower Arranging Societies (see below under United Kingdom for contract details).

WAFA's objectives are to reinforce the bonds between the various members and to promote the exchange of information concerning floral art interests. If you are interested in flower arranging as a hobby then do get in touch at the address given for your country – they will be able to help you further your interest in flowers.

**Argentina**
Mrs Susana Schiaffino
Peru 630-5-20
1068 Capitol Federal
Buenos Aires
Argentina

**Australia**
Mrs Norma Gordon
10 Balaka Street
Rosny
Tasmania
Australia

**Barbados**
The Barbados Flower
Arrangement Society
P.O. Box 8
Christchurch
Barbados
West Indies

**Belgium**
Belgian Flower
Arrangement Society
(B.F.A.S.)
Mrs Eliane Joski
Kortrijksesteenweg 834
B-9000-Gent
Belgium
E-mail:
BFAS@belgianflower.isabel.be

**Bermuda**
The Garden Club of
Bermuda
P.O. Box HM 1141
Hamilton HMEX
Bermuda
Tel: 1-441-293-2865

**Canada**
The Registry of Garden
Clubs of Canada
c/o Royal Botanical
Gardens
P.O. Box 399
Hamilton
Ontario L8N 3H5

**France**
Société Nationale
d'Horticulture de France
(SNHF–Floral Art)
Madame Jacqueline
Bogrand
84 rue de Grenelle
75007 Paris
France

**Hong Kong**
Hong Kong Flower Club
GPO Box 11991
Hong Kong

**India**
Pushpa Bitan Friendship
Society
Mrs Kavita Poddar
10 Dover Park,
Calcutta 700019
India

**International**
International Design
Symposium Ltd
64 Churchill Road
Westwood
MA, 02090–1602
USA
E-mail: kennstep@erols.com

**Ireland**
IEFA
Nuala Hegarty
96 Brookwood Avenue
Dublin 5
Ireland

**Italy**
Instituto Italiano per la
Decoraziano Floreale per
Amatori (IIDFA)
Mrs Rosnella Cajello Fazio
P.O. Box 229
18038 San Remo
Italy
Tel/Fax: 00 39 0184
575779

**Jamaica**
Jamaica Panel of Judges of
Floral Art and Horticulture
P.O. Box 203
Kingston 8
Jamaica

**Japan**
Nipon Flower Designers
Association
4-5-6 Takanawa
Minato-ku
Tokyo 108-8585
Japan

**Kenya**
Kenya Floral Arrangement
Club
Mrs Veena Sagoo
P.O. Box 6670
Nairobi
Kenya

**Korea**
Korea International Floral
Arts and Crafts
Development Association
Flora Suok Seoh
C.P.O. Box 4078
Seoul 100-640
South Korea

**Malta**
The Malta Floral Club
57 Sir Luigi Camilleri
Street
Sliema
SLM 12
Malta

**Mexico**
Federation Mexicana de
Jardineria y Arregio Floral
Mrs Sara Lambarri
ADPO Postal 41-842
Lomas Virreyes
Mexico DF 11000

**The Netherlands**
Nederlandse Amateur
Bloemschik Studieklub
(NABS)
Daisy de Vries Juncker
172 Tongerenseweg
8162 PP Epe
The Netherlands

**New Zealand**
The Floral Society of New
Zealand (FASNZ)
Mrs Byrta Wagsraff
3/207 Ocean Road
Mount Maunganui
New Zealand

**Pakistan**
Karachi Floral Art Society
Mrs Shahimah Sayeed
160c block 3
P.E.G.H.S.
Karachi, 75400
Pakistan

**Peru**
Club de Jardines del Para
'Floralies'
av Golf Los Incas 440
Las Villas del Golfo 11
Monterrico Surco
Lima 33
Peru

**Russia**
International Creative
Association of Flower
Arrangement Clubs, 'Artflora'
Mrs Nina A. Lozovaya
Gen. Ermolov str 12,28
Moscow 121293

**Republic of South Africa**
South Africa Flower Union
P.O. Box 1
Philloppolis 9970
Free State

**South Africa**
South African Floral
Institute (SAFU)
Kim Zimmerman
SAFU Secretary
33 Cyprus Road
Somerset West
South Africa 7130
E-mail: alanz@synapp.co

**Switzerland**
The Swiss Association of
Flower Arrangers
Mrs Susan Hafner
88 Chemin de Ruth
1223 Cologny-Geneve 2
E-mail:
lhafner@worldcom.ch

**United States of America**
The Garden Club of
America
14 East 60th Street
3rd Floor
New York, NY 10022
E-mail: hq@gcamerica.org

**United Kingdom**
National Association of
Flower Arrangement
Societies (NAFAS)
Osborne House
12 Devonshire Square
London EC2M 4FE
Tel: 00 44 207 247 5567
Fax: 00 44 207 247 7232
E-mail:
flowers@nafas.org.uk
Website: www.nafas.org.uk

**Uruguay**
The Garden Clubs of
Uruguay
Audrey T. Gonzalez
Rambla Tomas Berreta
6725
Monte Video
C.P. 11500
Uruguay 11500
E-mail:
audrey@chasque.apc.org

**Zimbabwe**
National Association of
Garden Clubs of Zimbabwe
Ms Patricia West
173 Dandro village
Emerald Hill
Harare
E-mail:
johnmus@icon.co.zw

# International Flower Schools

**Belgium**
Daniel Ost
O-L-Vrouwplein 26
Sint Niklaas 9100
Tel: 00 32 3776 1715
Fax: 00 32 3778 1358

**Czech Republic**
Stredni Zahradnicka Skola
Poabi 471 CZ-276 87
Melnik

**France**
Guy Martin
Centre International de
Formation d'Art Floral
6 rue de la Republique
60810 Villers Saint
Frambourg
Tel: 00 33 3 44 54 43 51
Fax: 00 33 3 44 54 44 85

Monique Gautier
École Française de
Decoration Florale
8 rue du General Bertrand
75007 Paris
Tel: 00 33 1 349652
Fax: 00 33 1 40 563872
E-mail: efdf@libertysurf.fr

**Germany**
Gregor Lersch
Telegraphenstrasse 9
Postfach 100738
D-5483
Bad Neuenahr
Tel: 00 49 2641 7047
*Groups Only*

**Greece**
Angeliki Kokkinoy
15 AG Konstantinou Str.
18532 Piraeus
Tel: 00 30 14170282
Fax: 00 30 14125443

**Hong Kong**
Tonie Yuen
Unit 12B
Hua Chiao Commercial
Centre
678 Nathan Road
Kowloon
Hong Kong
Tel: 852 2395 3599
Fax: 852 2395 3590
E-mail:
tonie@tonieyuen.com.hk

**Italy**
I.I.D.F.A.
P.O. Box 229
18038 San Remo
Tel/Fax: 00 39 0184575779

**Japan**
Manako Flower Academy
Roppongi City Building 2F
3-1-25 Roppongi
Minato-ku
Tokyo 106-0082
Tel: 00 81 3 5563 7844
Fax: 00 81 3 5563 7845
E-mail: manako@big.or.jp
Website:
www12.big.or.jp/-manako

Yutaka Jimbo
Ohya Building 302
2-9-3 Kyonan-cho
Masashino-City
Tokyo 180-0023
Tel: 00 81 4223 44601

Nippon Flower Designers
Association
4-5-6 Takanawa
Minatu-ku
Tokyo 108
Tel: 00 81 3542 08741

**Korea**
Chun Won Lee
No. 650-21, Balsan 2 Dong
Kangsu-ku
Seoul
Tel: 00 822 2366 11710

**The Netherlands**
Aad Van Uffelen at Holland
College
Chrysant 1
2678 PA
De Lier, Holland
Website:
www.holland-college.nl

**New Zealand**
Heather Hammond
Oturu Road
RD2 Otorhanga
Waikato
Tel/Fax: 00 647 873 0824

**Norway**
Nils Iversen and Rolf
Torhaug
Kreativ Flora
N.Slottsgt 8
N-0517, Oslo
Tel: 00 47 22 42 2722

**Spain**
Luis Lopez Barreto
Escuela Andaluza de Arte
Floral
41110 Bollulos de la
Mitacion
Seville
Tel: 00 349 9557 65295

**Taiwan**
Susita Flower Academy
94726 Bangna Complex
Bangna Trad Road
Prakamong
Bangkok 10260

China Floral Art
Foundation
No. 6 Alley 17, Lane 111
Fu-Hsing South Road
Sec. 2, Taipei 106 R.O.C.

**United Kingdom**
Judith Blacklock Flower
School, Knightsbridge
4/5 Kinnerton Place South
London SW1X 8EH
Tel: 00 44 207 235 6235
Fax: 00 44 207 235 6335
E-mail:
school@judithblacklock.com
Website:
www.judithblacklock.com

Japanese Floral and Garden
Design
21 Queens Gate Place
Mews
London SW7 5DG
Tel: 00 44 207 584 7662
Website:
www.takashisawano.co.uk

Ikebana Teachers
Association
Tricia Hill
Cornhill House
The Hangers
Bishops Waltham
Hants SO32 1EF
Tel: 00 44 1489 892656

The Studio @ Montford
Cottage
Fence, Nr. Burnley
Lancs BB12 9NZ
Tel/Fax: 00 44 1282
603220
E-mail:
thestudio@montford.
p3online.net

**United States of America**
The American Floral Art
School
529 Wabash
Suite 610
Chicago
IL. 60605
Tel: 00 1 312 922 9328

Floral Design Institute
911 Western Avenue
Suite 575
Seattle
Washington
Tel: 00 1 206 749 9464
Fax: 00 1 206 749 9374
Email: leanne@floraldesign
institute.com
Website:
www.floralschool.com

The Flower Arranging
Study Group of the Garden
Clubs of America
Ruth Crocker
120 Avon Hill Street
Cambridge
MA 02140
USA

International Design
Symposium Ltd
64 Churchill Road
Westwood
MA 02090–1602
USA
E-mail: kennstep@erols.com

Rittners School of Floral
Design
345 Marlborough Street
Boston
MA. 02115
Tel: 00 1 617 267 3824
E-mail: stevrt@tiac.net
Website:
www.floralschool.com

This list is not, of course, exhaustive. If you would like to be mentioned in
the next edition of *Teach Yourself Flower Arranging* please contact the author at
The Judith Blacklock Flower School, Knightsbridge,
4/5 Kinnerton Place South, London SW1X 8EH.

# Index